The ins and Outs of "Jack" Entrepreneurship

The Perspectives of "Jacks" (aka Generalists) as entrepreneurs and Employees are Changing- Jack's Impacts are Far More Significant Than Specialist's When Engaged with New Knowledge

Interviewers Do not Miss Out on Jack's Contributions!

Written and Edited by: Kristene Crooks

A successful entrepreneur, innovator, forward-thinker, strategic analysist, trainer, and all things business consulting.

<u>TABLE OF CONTENTS</u>

Chapter 1- Jacks and Specialists

My entire life, I referred to myself as a "jack of all trades but a master of none." It was not until my junior year of college (pursuing my third degree- all being in majorly different areas) that I learned several employers consider these "jacks" as negatively contributing employees! I was so shocked by this perspective; I had NEVER imagined that this could even be considered harmful to your professional reputation. After all, isn't it more beneficial to have a vast knowledge? A "jack of all trades but a master of none" means someone can do various things but are not particularly good at any one of them. People often refer to a jack of all trades as a person who lacks the focus and determination to stick to one thing; instead, they keep hopping from one task to another. It is used negatively as a derogatory remark.

I am afraid I must disagree with this negative view of a jack of all trades. I do not feel that the person who knows several things is due to lack of capability, lack of skills, incompetency, or a lack of focus; they are generalists. They are just passionately curious about everything! Common, well-known generalists include- Elon Musk, Steve Jobs, Leonardo DaVinci. A jack of all trades is a generalist. Some theories suggest that entrepreneurs MUST be generalists to succeed, while other theories suggest that entrepreneurs be specialists to succeed. Individuals are often not generalists; instead, they were taught to focus on one area of expertise. They do not explore other possibilities due to fear of stability, security, or just only because "it is not right to do that."

Not focusing on several areas can be detrimental to an entrepreneur's "big picture" way of thinking. Becoming a "jack of all trades" allows an entrepreneur to know more, fuel the imagination or passion, jolt creativity, and overall heighten the ability to succeed. "Jacks," we will refer to them as, are always seeking to "add a new feather to their hat," sometimes making them just as valuable as an entire team of experts.

Both approaches, specialist, and jacks, offer their credibility and benefits to entrepreneurs' lives.

Chapter 2- Entrepreneurship and Jacks

When first starting a business, for it to be successful, an entrepreneur must be skilled in several areas during the first few years, especially. It is highly unlikely and rare that a single entrepreneur possesses all of the predictable skills for an entrepreneur's success; however, the more that the generalist entrepreneur does possess, the more likely they will be successful in their ventures. Jack's personality mentality of "easily switching topics of interest and pursue" also can be seen a favorable for the theory of entrepreneurship known as radical subjectivist theory.

Ludwig Lachmann developed the radical subjectivist theory. Lachmann suggested that entrepreneurs develop plans according to their subjective knowledge and expectations. Theorist, Lachmann, assumes "individuals experience time differently, and the only way to interpret events is to reconstruct them from bits of information after they have occurred." A person's knowledge develops according to their interpretations of the past and their expectations for the future. As with everyone, including entrepreneurs, our interpretations and expectations are always changing, developing, and growing as we move through life. For this reason, entrepreneurs or jacks should embrace their continuous revision of plans.

Many potential "jack" entrepreneurs chose not to pursue their ventures due to controversies associated with them not "specializing" in any area, suggesting they are not credible enough in any particular area to create a profit. The uncertainty bearing theory of entrepreneurship, developed by Frank Knight, attempted to explain the 'phenomena of entrepreneurship.' Knight suggested that the uncertainties that come with entrepreneurship ventures create more profit, the higher the uncertainty, the higher the profit. There is a significant amount of emphasis placed on an entrepreneur's ability to make decisions under uncertainty. He suggested that those who do take on more significant uncertainty situations are the ones who deserve greater profit shall they succeed. The greater an entrepreneur's self-confidence, the more they can take on; their uncertainty is according to individual inclinations and abilities. The theory suggests that uncertainty can be reduced if it is pooled among serval entrepreneurs, aka among several areas of expertise or knowledge. This suggests that if an entrepreneur does have more knowledge areas, their ability to take on higher amounts of uncertainty will be more remarkable. Additionally, the more someone knows – about several different areas and topics- generally induces a greater sense of self-confidence, suggesting they will be able to tolerate higher degrees of uncertainty successfully.

While being a Jack can be greatly beneficial, there are also downfalls to entrepreneurship contributions if it is not "done correctly." Jacks are those who have knowledge and skills in several areas; however, they are also known as being a "master of none." A Jack that does try to be a "Master" of several things could spread themselves too thinly and ultimately halt operations. The 'ability to wear several hats' is a greatly beneficial quality. Jacks can think on their feet, react to problems quickly, and make more informed business decisions. Jacks need to focus on the skills they are offering, contributing to the business's uniqueness rather than attempting to be great at EVERYTHING their competitors offer, which is a common trait of a Jack- to learn to secure all skills they come across. Another downfall of Jack's is that they often feel like they can learn anything and do it all themselves. There are benefits to not being afraid to admit you may not be the best in one business area and pay to outsource that area. Investing in your business is vital to its overall success and growth. Jacks are often misrepresented in the working world.

Chapter 3- Jacks and Employment

Often even in the working world, human resources managers and supervisors have extremely negative connotations of Jacks. Employers miss out on significant valuable assets when they overlook generalists and only prefer specialists in their workforce. A broad range of interests, experimenting, and changing course now and then are essential to one finding their true passion. How would one know what they are passionate about if they have not considered it, tried it, or experienced it? If someone has only experienced one thing, how do they know they are passionate about something? How is it decided if one is only used to something or genuinely passionate? How does experiencing one area allow them to see their passion? Do specialists never actually experience the passion and are ignorant of the true meaning of passion? "Sampling periods" allow one to gain a broad skill set used later to specialize in a newly found passion. Jacks learn about their interests and abilities while their peers are plateauing at lower levels of their earlier specializations. Jacks often have a more comprehensive skill set, which affords them the flexibility needed to respond to situations they have never seen using their vast array of flexible skills. "Breadth of training predicts the breadth of the transfer." The more varied one's training, knowledge, and skills, the more able they will be to apply skills to situations they have never experienced before flexibly—those who 'specialize' in something experience repetitive work patterns associated with their specialization. Jacks are experienced in several skill sets, have experiences in several unexpected and nonrepetitive environments that provide them with the ability and skill that specialists do not have, responding to new and unforeseen situations. It is not that Jacks will never be specialists. However, they take the time to experience several things to better understand their true passion, which they often become entrepreneurs in. Because they know they are passionate about their late sprouted choice of specialization, Jacks will lead longer careers than those who specialize from the get-go leading to boredom more quickly and leaving their field. Those who immediately specialize more quickly surpass Jacks regarding income and success; Jacks far surpass early specializers once they determine their passion for specialization following their sampling period. The reason being, Jacks are genuinely passionate about their specialization, so they do not bore with it as quickly, and they excel further due to their true passion.

As the rumored suggestion says, generalists do not lack focus; instead, they set themselves up to excel in the workforce. Although they are skilled in several areas, most generalists do not do "half-a$#@d" work in those areas; instead, they pride themselves on excellence in all the areas they possess skill sets. Generalists/Jacks are more likely to achieve higher success levels due to their broad knowledge base and overall understanding of operations and functions. The term "multihyphenate" arose in recent years, coined to refer to those having several professions or businesses going at once. The generations replacing the retiring baby boomer's generation are becoming Jacks on purpose, and they are doing it for career success! The new "Job-Hopping Movement" of millennials is to learn opportunities and fulfill their desire to succeed and work-life balance that they "value more than previous generations." Companies are changing perspectives on 'ideal' job applicants.

Jacks/Generalists, due to the recent changing perspectives of employers, are continuously proving they are the strongest candidates rather than the conventional thought of "bad negative candidates." Significant skills generalists possess that specialists lack= they have learned repeatedly how to adapt. In today's ever-changing society and marketplace. a company's ability to adapt is crucial if not dependent on its ability to adapt. Jacks possess the ability to pivot strategies in the face of unforeseen problems with greater ease. The diversity and experience with several different groups of consumers, employees, and coworkers better prepare Jacks to communicate effectively with any team members. Having a flexible skill set in today's marketplace is crucial. Generalists are innovators; several 'specialist companies' today are failing due to their inability to innovate.

Recent research results have proven that Jacks not only end up doing things earlier than specialists, but their impact is far more significant when engaged with new knowledge. When new things arise, Jacks are often the first to try the new offerings vs. specialists who use what works and what they know. Jacks are more likely to think outside of the proverbial box; they are more likely to discover something genuinely new and innovative. Useless knowledge can always come in handy, often at the most unexpected times. Previously, to advance in a career, a person needed to specialize and become an expert in an area.

Chapter 4- Modern Economies and Jacks

Today's vast growing global economy brings several
uncertainties and unrelated developments to businesses.
Generalists are simply better at navigating uncertainty.
Generalists are also better at predictions of business ventures
then specialists. "When seeking accuracy of predictions, it is
better to turn to those who know many little things, draw from an
eclectic array of traditions, and accept ambiguity and
contradictions." Today's situations are often vaguer and more
undefined than they were 20 years ago; therefore, specialists
who depend upon a single perspective end up being detrimental
to their navigation in today's economy. In today's uncertain
environment, "a breadth of perspectives, such as those that

Jacks hold, trump breadth of knowledge." While it is right specialists have several things to offer, Jacks' conventional perspective of bringing nothing compared to the table is dissipating, and the table is turning. Jacks create more flexible labor forces, and by being skilled in numerous functions, they are more valuable to management as they can dynamically adjust roles. Several of today's forward-looking companies are making it a requiring multifunctional experience mandatory for career progression. Analytical abilities, such as necessary statistical skills and reasoning abilities, are more desired than domain-specific skill sets in today's global economy.

Innovation is what drives today's economy. Do you think a specialist CEO, or a Jack CEO would be better at leading their organization in innovation? Why? While both can innovate, the generalist CEO's strategies will most likely have the most significant impact, originality, and generality for the organization. Jacks have often worked in several different positions, industries, and firms, which equipped them with the general knowledge that proves useful to transformative change. One of the critical challenges in today's changing knowledge-based economy for organizations regarding innovation is creating their firms without boundaries. Many of today's organizations seek horizontal networks linked through cross-functional teams and desire to form strategic alliances with all suppliers, customers, and competitors. Some companies choose to hire outside consultants who are Jacks to provide them with this innovative assistance for transformative innovation. Jacks are more likely to take a greater risk due to their broader set of outside options. Organizations led by Jacks also tend to have a more significant number of patents filed and more impactful innovation.

Today's organizations desire to be adaptable, flexible, efficient, flatter, less bound, and more networked. Jacks excel at connecting across several diverse domains and pursue problems with unclear parameters. Sound judgment and broad perspective are valuable assets of Jacks needed to make sound forecasts and decisions. The overspecialization of individuals acts as a barrier, robbing them of the ability to see what is directly in front of them and of common-sense views. Standard- sense views, rather than specialized competence, is needed to predict things. Yesterday's management referred to Jacks as 'masters of nothing' when Jacks are mastering several specialties accumulating more global multilayered understandings that are desirable of today's management. Organizations previously eliminated possible opportunities for managers to learn all aspects of the business, which drove the organization's struggle to perform. With their vast array of knowledge, Jacks have learned several, if not all, aspects of a business. Jacks are especially useful in today's slow economy.

They are cross-functional with multiple skills that eliminate the need for as many employees, saving companies money in the long run. Dipesh Lall, a director of information management and analytics, can be quoted as saying, "The ability to connect the proverbial dots will always be a superior skill to painting each dot perfectly. Higher-order problems require strong generalist ability and an abiding willingness to tolerate and temper ambiguity".

Jacks can survive just about anywhere they go, while specialists can only survive under certain limited situations only when they are perfect. The culture is changing to being a data-rich and meaning poor society; it is becoming essential to know "a little about a lot," which Jacks will thrive in. Like how specialists can only reveal some truths… some truths can only be revealed by a Jack. Specialists are single-minded. There are several different personality traits in comparison with generalists to specialists.

Chapter 5- Jack's Personality Traits/ Myers-Briggs Type Indicator Test

Personality traits are used as determinants for employers in the hiring process to fulfill certain positions. The Myers-Briggs Type Indicator test is well known in the U.S. and is often used to determine prospective employees' dominant characteristics. Other companies find a use for this test as a management development tool to better their managers visualize employees' perspectives. The test categorizes 16 different stereotypes based on a person's four most dominant personality characteristics. The test focuses on eight specific personality characteristics: extrovert, introvert, sensing, intuitive, thinking, feeling, perceiving, and judging. Sensing individuals often find joy in seeking out details. Intuitive individuals often have an impeccable "sixth sense" and focus on bigger pictures. Thinkers are more logical and objective. Feelers are more subjective and think with their hearts more. Perceivers find joy in collecting information and apply that collected information using flexible methods. Judgmental individuals enjoy decision making responsibilities and tend to get things done. The test asks a series of 100 questions devised to determine how individuals conduct themselves in different situations. It is currently the most widely used personality test.

The results of individuals that have taken the Myers-Briggs Type Indicator personality test produced several conclusions that employers often use as a hiring tool.

The smallest percentage of tested individuals, mostly chief executives, possess the four most significant introversion characteristics: intuition, thinking, and judgmental. They are often highly creative and original individuals with an exceptional drive. People often describe them as skeptical, critical, independent, determined, stubborn, and have a knack for getting their agendas accepted by others.

- Those that were found more likely to become entrepreneurs possessed the chief characteristics of extroversion, intuition, thinking, and perceiving. Perceived as quick, ingenious, generalists, resourceful at solving difficult problems, and neglect routine tasks.

- Chief Financial Officers tend to possess introversion, sensing, thinking, and judging.

- Engineers often possess introversion, sensing, thinking, and perception.

- Researchers often possess introversion, sensing, feeling, and perception. Often perceived as caring, inquisitive learners, independent, friendly, and absorbed.

- Operations and staff personnel often possess extroverted, sensing, thinking, and judging. They are often perceived as practical, realistic, matter-of-fact individuals, have a natural head for business details, and like to organize/run activities.

- Sales People often possess sensing, feeling, perception, extroversion. Perceived as outgoing, easygoing, empathetic, and friendly; enjoy entertaining, sports, and making things, often remembering facts over understanding theories.

- Generalists often possess introversion, intuition, thinking, and judging. Will get the job done 'anyway.' Are conductors. Know how far to go too far. "Never walk out on a rope unless they have a safety net in place."

- Specialists often possess extroversion or introversion, thinking, perceiving, feeling, sensing, and judging. They often try to get the job done 'their way.' Are soloists. Prone to go too far. "Are like tight rope walkers who get halfway out on the rope before they realize they are tight, and the rope is not."

Chapter 6- Forward Looking Business Models and Jacks

The basis for a forward-looking business model is to develop the corporate culture further. A leadership style focusing on outcomes rather than the amount of time a person spends inside their office is required. Companies should seek to be perceived as a flexible and attractive employer, motivate employees, and improve company performance capabilities. A people-first attitude is becoming foundational for corporate cultures. Furthermore, good company culture is key to success.

Flexibility, especially enlighten of the COVID 19 Pandemic, is crucial to navigation and should be the center of all corporate cultures at this time. The pandemic has enticed what some call an "era of agility,", extending remote working opportunities and making it a benchmark of several organizational activities. COVID 19 forced many organizations to reevaluate their corporate culture. Awareness is what leads to change. Several organizations only associate flexibility with working from home; this is not so. Innovation and creative ventures must be considered to offer flexibility to frontline workers as well. To continue attracting skilled employees, employers need to adjust cultures and devise new ways of thinking.

Generalists can be the answer to the need for adjusting cultures and devising new ways of thinking. Jacks see the 'big picture' from an outside the box perspective. Jacks possess a breadth of transferable skills, which are becoming crucial in today's workforce. Jacks possess skill sets required for management such as effective communication and good people skills; regardless of the industry, these are essential to leading, whether it be accountants or retail salespersons. Job climates are rapidly changing. Both generalists and specialists face the threat of automatization. Robots or specific programs can completely do certain jobs. Those facing the most massive threat in today's economy are specialists. They have the narrowest skillset and may need even to re-educate if their job is threatened. Specialist jobs are most threatened by automation because the activities are repetitive. The future may even hold a place for generalizing specialists or specializing generalists. A generalizing specialist "starts as a generalist but also has in-depth knowledge over a particular area." A specializing generalist is a "specialist in a particular field that also has a broader understanding of other aspects of the business." These options offer the 'best of both worlds.' Regardless of specialist or generalist- they are both essential to a workplace and should both be valued. Passion is needed for success- an individual should pursue the option that best fulfills their passions.

Chapter 7- Comparisons of Specialists and Jacks

Neither specialists nor jacks are better than one or the other. The differences are not a matter of intellectuals or abilities. Both specialists and jacks require hard work, dedication, and passion for succeeding. Whether you are a jack or specialist is often dependent upon your personality and your drive. Regardless of what you are- with hard work, determination, and passion, you can succeed. Both provide significant disadvantages and advantages to not only the entrepreneurial world but the workforce as well. Just as eggs' perspective, going from being good for you to being bad for you back to being good for you- the 'perspective' of specialists or jack entrepreneurial is dependent on the current trends and times. Something once viewed as 'bad' yesterday can be viewed as 'good' tomorrow with a change of circumstances, the introduction of new views, and new perspectives brought to the table. Do not let the theories and studies determine your future; you are the only one whom you can determine your future. Whether you are a jack or specialist, if you want to become an entrepreneur, by all means- chase your dreams.

Chapter 8- Jacks Pursuing Business Ventures

Possibly several jacks do not pursue ventures due to the typical perspective they would not be successful. Entrepreneurs are, in fact, those that innovate and change the world. If more Jacks did not let perspectives chase them from pursuing ventures, they would create new perspectives and theories, as entrepreneurs do, leading to a domino effect of Jacks pursuing entrepreneurial ventures. "Being an agent of change means going against the status quo, and that requires a unique combination of idealism, grit, and determination." Bill Drayton, a social entrepreneurship pioneer, once said, "the first step to becoming a changemaker (the only secure job going forward) is to give one's self permission to ignore all those that say 'do not do it.'"

No two individuals have ever been nor ever will be exactly alike as everyone's personality is unique, which alters their perceptions of different experiences and how one responds to experiences. There is no 'one size fits all' guideline to success or determine if one should be/is/will be a successful entrepreneur. No matter how intelligent a person may be, they will not be successful without ambition and passion. Likewise, no matter how ambitious and passionate you are, it will be tough to succeed if you lack the necessary intelligence. Others simply possess incredible amounts of luck.

Chapter 9- The Changing Economy Demands New Rules, Procedures, and Precedence…… What Used to Work Is No Longer Working

The economy is changing. What used to work is not working anymore. Entrepreneurs need to stand against the mediocracy of doing what everyone else is doing; stop using old rules and procedures for new successes. New precedence needs to be set. There must be some that are willing to go against cultural norms and stop taking the 'easy defined way.'

New economies require new strategies, new rules, new procedures, new 'way to do things,' and new success. Actual change requires a bold determination and a willingness to see outside of the defined box. The search for outside confirmation, validation, and individuals doubting themselves for their bold new approaches needs to cease so they can be transformed into change. You must believe in the things you cannot see and do things that you have not done before to inspire and create change. Change is never an easy venture, but; nothing worth having will ever come easy.

Chapter 10- How Jacks Can Change the Business World

Entrepreneurs seek change. That is just what they are. There are several challenges, setbacks, and struggles to achieve a purpose and change the world to reflect your vision, but they can be overcome by allowing your deep passion for pushing you through. Throughout society's history, there have been several instances when individuals have defied the 'norms' and conventional practices to introduce their visions, which ended up becoming 'norms' and conventional practices. Take Henry Ford; for example, he invented the automobile. Ford designed his business model, which he named Fordism – "the mass production of inexpensive goods coupled with workers' high wages." Ford introduced the, now traditional, five-day work week. The corporation, known as 'B Corp,' a legal business structure, did not exist until recently; it developed from entrepreneurs creating new business structures. Society is always changing. While it is smart and essential to do your research on entrepreneurship, you should not allow your research findings to divert you from your path of pursuing your ventures. Perhaps you will be the next individual that does not conform to conventional perceptions of ('who has what it takes to become an entrepreneur?'/ 'will I become a successful entrepreneur?'/ or 'how do I become an entrepreneur?') entrepreneurship and successfully establish a massive organization that is the footprint for the future of entrepreneurship, organizational structure, and 'norms' of this 'new economy' we are living in today.

Chapter 11- Types of Entrepreneurs

Entrepreneurship concepts are subject to your interpretations. There are several different 'current types' of entrepreneurs; remember these are CURRENT that does not mean these are THE types of entrepreneurs, as entrepreneurship has no boundaries. Some of the SEVERAL types of entrepreneurs include innovators, hustlers, imitators, researchers, and buyers. Each type is associated with different 'rules for success.' Maybe you will change tomorrow's entrepreneur types and define the 'rules for success' in this new age economy. Each already established type is associated with specifically defined characteristics, roles, and affects business success differently.

Innovators are the entrepreneurs that have developed entirely new ideas and use the newly developed ideas to create viable businesses. Most often, their presented ideas change how people think and do things. Their business idea most often drives innovators' motivation; they are incredibly passionate about the obsessive border. Innovators also use product differentiation strategies in finding creative new ways to market their idea, which allows their business to stand out as unique among their crowd of competitors. In extreme cases, their business surpasses standing out from the crowd of competitors and reaches the level of ultimately creating an entirely 'new crowd.' There are several advantages to being an innovator, including creating the rules, receiving all the success glory, and initially having minimum competition. Some disadvantages to innovators include needing significant amounts of capital to bring new ideas to life, resistance from shareholders, and the timeframe for success is longer.

Hustlers are entrepreneurs that work hard and are not afraid to 'get their hands dirty.' Hustlers often begin their ventures small while focusing on future growth. Fulfilling dreams is often the motivation for hustlers. Hustlers are often intensely focused and favor risks over comfort. Advantages to being a hustler often include often outworking others, have thick skin, not allowing them to give up quickly, and view disappointment or rejections as steppingstones in the process. There are also disadvantages to being a hustler, including being more prone to burn out; team members with lower work ethics quickly wear out. They often do not see raising capital as having a higher value than working harder.

Imitators are entrepreneurs that use other business ideas already established and tweak them to improve upon them slightly. Imitators are continually scanning the market, searching for ways to make products better than using their revisions to gain 'the upper hand' in the market. Imitators are a hybrid of hustlers and innovators; they do not live by already established terms, and they have significantly high self-confidence. The advantages of being an imitator include: it is more comfortable and less stressful to refine already established business ideas; it is accessible to benchmark performances, and you can use the originator as a template to avoid mistakes or learn. Disadvantages of being an imitator include: their ideas are not original; ideas are always compared to the originator, and they are always playing 'catch-up' rather than leading.

Researchers are entrepreneurs who analyze their ideas from every possible angle. They take their time to critically research all information that may be relevant to their idea. Failure is not an option for researchers, and they believe their business will be extraordinarily successful because they strive to understand all aspects of it. Researchers build their foundation for the business upon a deep understanding that results in a too long time to launch products and make decisions—instincts and intuition and not nearly as relevant as facts and data for researchers. Advantages of being a researcher include: they plan for as many contingencies as possible; they have detailed well thought out business plans and financial plans; they do not rely on gut feeling but instead rely on data and information; they will not initiate into a market until they feel they know the market, and the chance of failure is minimized. There are also disadvantages to being a researcher, including moving very slowly; they can sometimes lose sight of business operations and primarily focus on numbers, and they do not like the risk that could harm their new venture.

Buyers are entrepreneurs who are defined by wealth. Buyers generally have a significant amount of money and specialize in purchasing profitable businesses already established. They identify businesses, analyze its viability, acquire the business, and hire someone to run operations and grow the business. Advantages of being a buyer include already established ventures are less risky; innovation is not a significant concern; they do not have to focus on building the foundation and can focus on just building the business. There is already a market for the products. There is a disadvantage to being a buyer. The cost of a profitable business is generally exceedingly high, and the business you buy could have problems that you thought you could turn around, but you cannot.

Chapter 12- Forms of Entrepreneurship

There are many different forms of entrepreneurship. Forms of entrepreneurship include administrative, opportunistic, acquisitive, incubate, private, public, individual, mass, small business, large company, scalable startup, social, intrapreneurship, technopreneurship, cultural, international, ecopreneurship's, agriprenuership, transperenurship, commercial, E-entrepreneurship, domestic, trading, state, and joint entrepreneurship. The categories of entrepreneurship are based on the different activities associated with the venture.

Administrative entrepreneurship is defined by the administrative techniques and functions used to manage all current and future business situations with merits and a competitive edge. Examples include management of quality, redesigning jobs; new techniques to do things; and management by consensus. All activities within this category should maximize the organization's efficiency, nuke achievements, and sustain in the competitive marketplace.

Opportunistic entrepreneurship is defined by opportunities arising due to environmental changes. The opportunities are not easily recognized or able to be pursued timely by all owners in the industry. They are the first to identify, exploit, and perform otherwise unforeseen opportunities.

Acquisitive Entrepreneurship- uses collections of features and skills to allow and improve business efficiency and other competencies. Equips something new in value and accomplishes the capabilities technically. Something that would help sustain competitively. - They are encouraged to figure out such new things continuously.

Incubate Entrepreneurship- The generation of new ideas and ventures within the premises of an organization. Manages them in productive ways and ensures the material gain for the business.

Private Entrepreneurship- entrepreneurship initiated under the private sector—speeds economic development. The government gives support services to private and public to motivate private ventures.

Public entrepreneurship- initiated under the government through development agencies. They work under the government to solve public and environmental issues. Not social because government rules and regulations bound them.

Individual Entrepreneurship- managed and executed by an individual or family member with personal motives and initiatives.

Mass Entrepreneurship- there is a much favorable climate of encouragement and motivation among common masses.

Small Business Entrepreneurship- profit is the main reason behind them. Make up the most significant number of businesses within society. Employ up to 50% of the entire US workforce.

Large Company Entrepreneurship- most of them grow using innovation—finite life cycles found in them. Reasons for innovation are customization in customer demand, the establishment of new technologies, and new competitors' emergence. Create disruptive products or acquire innovative organizations. Disruptive innovation is hard to apply to large organizations.

Scalable startup Entrepreneurship- several people believe this is the same as a small business; they are different. The company starts with a vision to change the universe. Funding arises from venture capitalists. The main motive is to seek a scalable and repeatable business structure and look for more funding to grow. Not very many exist due to high risks.

Social Entrepreneurship- people, are innovators who target on development of products or services so social requirements and problems can be solved. The main motive is to improve the world.

Intrapreneurship- Foster activities of large organizations by making improvements in products and branding them to increase profits. Four elements= the right structure, qualified workforce, reward, collaboration for a bright future. Is incredibly significant in the changing world of competitiveness. Valuable assets are innovation and dedicated efforts by intrapreneur.

Technopreneurship- technology context and amalgamating entrepreneurial skills and technology where technology is an essential part. A new breed. Needs entrepreneur that's techno-savvy, creative, passionate, and with the ability to calculate risk in advance. IT plays an important role and provides resources for generating employment, utilizing resources, growth of technology, and creating capital.

Cultural Entrepreneurship- Entrepreneurs organize cultural, social, financial, and human capital to profit from it. Produce culturally right products, and generate opportunities for the economy, society, and culture. Motivation is the betterment of society by leveraging the business. At times, they lie to change the ideas, beliefs, and behaviors of people through communication and influence.

International Entrepreneurship- the whole process of entrepreneurship activities of business across boundaries of the nation. The highlighted purpose is to fulfill and satisfy the needs and wants of target audiences.

Ecopreneurship- aka- Green Entrepreneurship- Perspectives that signify corporations with the environment by working on their goals and profitability. They termed environmental entrepreneurship. They are concerned with the environment's problems while focusing on its operations and profit margin: 3 main concepts- eco-innovation, eco opportunity, and eco commitment.

Agriprenuership- Role played by agriculture in the growth of the economy and its development too. When an owner starts making improvements in agriculture, it includes all business operations such as manufacturing, production, and distribution of farm supplies. A type of farming business that includes the profitability, use of digital technologies to improve farming, farm management, and innovative solutions, and reduce waste of crops.

Transprenuership- groups of ppl from groups of gender like transgender or Hijra design small-scale businesses to fulfill their daily needs.

Commercial Entrepreneurship- only associated with profitability and emphasized on opportunities. Uses available resources lie between the hierarchies and handles the network on behalf of the entity. They are profit-based because all operations are held by taking profit as a significant motive. Focuses on the economy.

E-Entrepreneurship- aka Cyberprenuership- a world full of technology. Opportunities where individuals, organizations, society, and nations use mobile phones and computers to access online services. All owners try to shift to online businesses to get a reward from technology. Identifies and analyzes resources and converts them to online venture business. This sort of entrepreneur is known as SENs (Self employed entrepreneurs).

Domestic Entrepreneurship- The business owner produces good within the boundaries of a nation. Follow the rules and regulations established by the government of the country to grow domestically. Compiles with government policies, highly convenient, culturally sensitive, adapts to technologies, understands local systems, more opportunities for growth, risk, and reward.

Trading Entrepreneurship- Are mediators between the manufacturer of products and customers, retailers, or wholesalers. Serves as a middleman for dealers, wholesalers, manufacturers, and customers.

State Entrepreneurship- Business is managed and operated by the state or government of the state.

Joint Entrepreneurship- A collaboration of private and public entrepreneurship. A business is partly owned, controlled, and managed by a private entrepreneur and the government.

Chapter 13- How 'Old' Business Matters Should Be Viewed in the New Business Environment

As you can see, many already established categories have developed over the years pertinent to the types of entrepreneurs and categories of entrepreneurship. These already established categories should not act as barriers for potential entrepreneurs, but they should act as guidelines for things already innovated and established. The entrepreneur should try to seek ventures that surpass any already established categories/types to impact the world with their own 'footprint.'

If you desire to become an entrepreneur, there is no harm in trying to succeed. If you do not try, I guarantee you will never become an entrepreneur. It is essential that whatever venture you decide to pursue, it is something that you are passionate about. If you are pursuing something you genuinely care about, all of the hard work will be more bearable. Formal education is NOT required to become an entrepreneur. Some education (such as in business or areas related to specialties if required for your venture) can be precious. Creating a business plan is a precious asset to pursuing your venture also. Business plans layout in detail your objectives and strategies for accomplishing your objectives. Business plans are also critical if you are seeking funding for your venture. Business plans also provide a way for you to measure your success. Your target audience must be given significant consideration also. Your target audience's age, gender, income, race, and culture will all influence decisions regarding business operations, business locations, and marketing. By conducting significant research, you can best determine what target audience will best fit your business model; gear all operations to target your decided demographic. By establishing and maintaining a viable network, you create a support system that can help you find investors and support your business by sending you customers after operations. To be most successful, you must 'sell' your idea/product to your potential customers. Customers do not always know what they want; you need to devise a strategy that convinces them you offer the best available. Highlight things that make your product or service unique and the value it adds for individuals or organizations and uses these points to sell your product or service. If you become skilled at 'selling your idea,' you can succeed at any venture you devise. Marketing should be focused on before, during, and after operations begin. Through marketing, you inform your target audience of your existence, what you offer, and why they should choose your company. Focus all marketing efforts on your target audience. This may require some additional research. There is no 'best way' to become an entrepreneur; every experience will be different. There is no 'secret to success'; even the best business ideas can fail. With education, experiences, and extensive planning and research, you significantly increase the likelihood of succeeding. The population and diversity of populations are continually changing and increasing, which creates an even higher demand for new and better businesses.

There will always be a demand for entrepreneurs; however, not all fields chosen are equal in demand. The field you choose to pursue your venture in will significantly influence your success, potential max income earned, and job security.

Chapter 14- Planning Your Small Business – Market Research

<u>Market Research and Competitive Analysis</u>

You can validate and enrich your business idea and reduce risks through the use of market research. Market research involves researching consumer behaviors and economics trends. Demographic information research (age, wealth, family, interests, locations, race, religion, etc.) will help you understand potential opportunities and limitations referencing your target population.

-Questions that need to answer during market research:

1) **Demand**- is there a demand for or desire for your product or service idea?

2) **Market Size**- About how many people do you think would be interested in what you have to offer?

3)**Economic Indicators**- Find out your target audience income ranges and unemployment rates. This will give you a better understanding of their financial health.

4) **Location**- How far can your business reach, what are your target audience's locations?

5)**Market Saturation**- How many identical or similar options are already available to your target audience and your location.

6)**Pricing**- Price alternatives to your offering to get an idea of what customers would be willing to pay.

There are several methods to conduct your market research: you can use resources and data already compiled and available; you can conduct your surveys and research or go directly to your target audience. Resources readily available are the easiest, most convenient method, but the results may not be related to the information pertinent to your service or product idea; they may also not be directed toward only your target audience. Direct research can be expensive or time-consuming but can be very beneficial in assessing your logo, business name, business idea, demand, buying experiences, and to find out where customers are going to instead of your business and why.

Direct Research Methods:

-Surveys

-Questionnaires

-Focus Groups

-In-Depth Interviews

Chapter 15- Competitive Analysis

<u>**Competitive Analysis**</u>

The key to competitive analysis is identifying a competitive edge that will create significant revenue for your business. This analysis uses competing businesses as a learning resource for potential customers.

Things to Assess in the competitive landscape:

- Market share
- Strengths and weaknesses
- The window of opportunity to enter the market
- The importance of your target market to your competitors
- Barriers that could hinder you as you enter the market
- Indirect or secondary competitors that could impact your success

Industry Factors to Consider:

- Level of competition
- The threat of new competition or services
- Effect of suppliers and customers on price

<u>**Porter's Five Forces Analysis**</u>

Competition directly influences ANY business's level of success. Knowing who the competition is, how their services, products, and marketing strategies affect your business are crucial aspects of survival in today's market. Porter's Five

Forces model, a macro tool in business analytics that focuses on industries, is a way for businesses to understand their position within the industry and analyze the competition. Five factors/forces are analyzed to determine if your business idea will be profitable in the industry. Using this model better equips you to make significant, strategic decisions and to develop compelling competitive strategies.

1) **Competitive Rivalry**- This factor analyzes how intense the competition is, its number, and what each one can do. *High competition* = there are only a few competitors in a growing industry. Customers can easily switch to a competitor with little to no cost- advertising and price wars can happen, hurting your business's bottom line.

2) **Bargaining Power of Suppliers**- analyzes how much power suppliers have, how much control they have regarding the potential to raise their prices, which would hurt your company's profit potential. Analyzes how many suppliers there are and other available resources. *The fewer suppliers there are=, the more bargaining power they have. / Multiple suppliers and resources are better for businesses.*

3) **Bargaining Power of Customers**- Analyzes the power of customers and their effect on pricing and quality. *Customers have lower power when products are*

purchased in smaller amounts, and your product is significantly different or unique compared to competitors. / Customers have high power when there are few customers with several sellers.

4) **The threat of New Entrants**- Determines how easily or difficult it would be for a new company to enter the market. *The easier it is to enter= greater risk for your company due to market share depletion. Barriers include- absolute cost advantages, access to inputs, economies of scale, and strong brand identity.*

5) **The Threat of Substitute Products or Services**- Analyzes how easy it would be for a customer to switch from your product or service to a competitor. Considerations- the number of competitors, how their prices and quality compare to yours, the amount of profit competitors earn to determine if they can lower their costs even lower. *The threat of substitutes depends on switching long term and immediate costs and a customer's inclination to switch.*

Once all analyses have been conducted, you can review them in preparation for creating your strategy for competitive advantage.

Examples of Strategies:

- **Cost Leadership**- You could increase your profits by reducing your costs while charging industry-standard prices. You could also increase your market share by reducing sales prices while retaining profits.
- **Differentiation**- Your products or services offered must be significantly better/unique compared to your competitor's offerings. This not only improves your competitive position but also offers higher value to your customers. This requires thorough research, development, significant sales, and effective marketing.
- **Focus**- Requires an immanent understanding of your marketplace, sellers, buyers, and competitors. Use this understanding to select 'niche' markets to sell in.

The 'Sixth Force' to Consider (Complementors) Found in the 'Tools of Games Theory'

A complementor would be a company that offers products or services that, rather than compete with your company's offerings, complement your offerings. An example of this would be- you have a company that makes and sells arrows, and the complementor would be a company that makes and sells bows to shoot the arrows with. This factor is used to consider and explain strategic alliances rather than competition.

Once you have completed all the necessary analysis and research relevant to your business idea, you can create your business plan.

Chapter 16- Writing a Business Plan

Your business plan should act as your guide for starting, structuring, running, growing, and managing your business. Writing one can also help obtain needing funding; investors are always more intrigued when provided with a business plan.

There are two most common categories of business plans, traditional or lean startup.

-**Traditional Business Plans**- these are most common, use standard structure, and encourage detail to be provided for each section. The work effort is more significant upfront, and they are often several to dozens of pages in length. Lenders and investors will most often request this type of plan.

- **Lean Startup Business Plans**- These are less common, use standard structure, and focus on providing a summary only of crucial elements of your plan. If one is skilled in writing them, they can be completed in less than an hour and are often no longer than 1 page.

TRADITIONAL BUSINESS PLAN FORMAT

You can revise formats to fit your need. There is no right/wrong way to format your business plan. There are generally nine sections offered within the traditional business plan.

Section 1- Executive Summary

- Introduce your company and reasons for why you believe it will be successful.
- Include- mission statement, product or service, necessary information about your leadership team,

employees, financial information, high-level growth plans, and location.

Section 2- Company Description

- Provide a more detailed explanation of your company. Detail the problems you developed your company to solve.
- List consumers, organizations, and companies you intend to serve.
- Detail competitive advantages that will lead to your success and all of your strengths.

Section 3- Market Analysis

- Introduce all your findings from your market analysis and competitive research in this section.
- Identify trends and themes you discovered.
- Identify how you plan to do better than competitors, advantages competitors have, their strengths and weaknesses, why they are strengths and weaknesses, and what successful companies do.

Section 4- Organization and Management

- Introduce the legal structure of your company and who runs operations.
- Create an organizational chart to show who oversees the company visually.
- You can include resumes and cover letters of your key players.
- Define what each key player will 'bring to the table.'

Section 5- Service or Product Line

- Please describe the products you plan to sell or services you plan to offer, their benefits to customers, and the lifecycle of each.
- If conducting research and development- explain it in detail here.
- Discuss any patents or copyrights- any other intellectual property planning

Section 6- Marketing and Sales

- The marketing strategy is not definite- it should change/evolve to continuously fit your needs and your consumer's needs.
- Describe how you plan to attract and retain your customers.
- Describe the actual sale process.
- Thoroughly describe all strategies.

Section 7- Funding Requests

- Outline any funding requirements here.
- Introduce the amount of income you will need over the next five years and detail how the funding will be used.
- Specify- debt or equity funding, terms you would like applied, length of time your request covers, and a detailed description of how the funds will be used.
- Explain strategic financial plans
- Specify the reason you need funds

Section 8- Financial Projections

- Tell the financial story of your business here
- Use graphs or charts if you want.
- You are trying to convince others that your business is stable and will be financially successful here.

- If you have already established…, include- income statements, balance sheets, cash flow statements, and any collateral to be used against a loan.
- This should be a five-year financial outlook. Include- forecasted income statements, balance sheets, cash flow statements, and capital expenditure budgets.
- The first of the five years should be more detailed- use monthly or quarterly projections.

Section 9- Appendix

- Include supporting documents or materials requested in this section.
- Credit histories, resume, cover letters, product pictures, letters of recommendation, letters of reference, licenses, patents, legal documents, permits, contracts, etc.

<u>BUSINESS MODEL CANVAS- LEAN STARTUP BUSINESS PLAN FORMAT</u>

<u>*the oldest, most well-known template. These are charts used to describe a company's value, proposition, infrastructure, customers, and finances.</u>

9 Components of this model-

1) **Key Partnerships-**
- Suppliers, manufacturers, subcontractors, strategic partners

2) **Key Activities-**
- How you plan to gain a competitive advantage.

3) **Key Resources-**
- List resources that create value for customers.

4) **Value Proposition-**

- Create a clear and compelling statement that reflects the unique value you will bring to the market.
  5) **Customer Relations-**
- Describe your customer's experience from start to finish.
  6) **Customer Segments-**
- Identify your target audience.
  7) **Channels-**
- Identify how you will communicate with customers.
  8) **Cost Structure-**
- Define your strategy and the highest costs you will face pursuing it.
  9) **Revenue Streams-**
- Describe how your company will make money.

Chapter 17- Finding Funding

-Self Funding

- aka "bootstrapping"- use your 'pocket money' to fund your business. You can get the money from family members, friends, savings, and even borrowing from your 401K.

-Venture Capital from Investors

- investors fund you in the form of venture capital investments. This is generally offered in exchange for ownership shares and an active role within your

company. Typically, they- focus on high growth companies, invest in return for equity rather than debt (not a loan), take higher risks for the potential of higher returns, and have a longer investment time than traditional financing. Almost ALL investors will want a seat on the board of directors.
- How to get this funding- find an investor (look for individual investors- sometimes called 'angel investors' or venture capital firms), Share your business plan (this will be used to review to ensure it meets their investing criteria), go through a due diligence review (the investors will conduct a thorough analysis of your business), work out the terms (agree on a terms and conditions sheet), investment (get the investment)

- **Crowdfunding-**
- Raises funds from many people called crowd funders.
- They do not expect a financial return or any part of ownership or control
- They expect to receive a 'thank you gift' in return for their funds (often the product you plan to sell or perks
- It is a low risk for owners
- Every crowdfunding platform is different- ensure you read the fine print, so you understand your full financial and legal obligations

- **SBA Guaranteed Loans-**
- The SBA (Small Business Association) can guarantee loans that banks believe to be too risky. This takes a significant amount of risk away from the bank, and they are more willing to offer to fund.

- **Small Business Investment Companies-**
- These are privately owned investment funds that are licensed and regulated by the SBA. They use their capital and funds borrowed with an SBA guarantee to make equity and debt investments to qualifying small businesses.

- **Small Business Innovation Research Program-**
- A program that encourages small businesses to engage in federal research and development provides the potential for commercialization.

- **Small Business Technology Transfer Program-**
- Offers to fund for federal innovation research and development arena.

- **Grants-**
- There are several grants offered to small businesses. The SBA offers funding programs, and some federal grants are available for scientific research and development. There are grants offered to companies that assist with export development. Federal grants are often offered to (nonprofits, educational institutions, state, and local governments), nonprofits/state/and local governments also offer some grants directly to small businesses

- **Activities that raise money-**
- You can also participate in activities that will raise money to put toward your business ventures- such as writing a book! (I started writing books to aid individuals regarding business matters in consulting and raise money for business ideas/ventures that I hope to pursue).

Chapter 18- Entrepreneurship is a Lifestyle

Now that you grasp the basics of modern-day entrepreneurship, we can discuss the potential benefits you could experience while pursuing your venture. It is not ALL struggle and hardships becoming an entrepreneur. Being an entrepreneur is not a job; instead, it is a lifestyle. You have a flexible schedule as you create your schedule. Having more control over your work leads to job satisfaction, being more engaged, and being less emotionally exhausted. You have the ability and privilege to structure your company to be in line with your core values and career values. The path to being an entrepreneur is a path of continuous improvement of your skillset. "Fake it til you make it," one of my favorite sayings is describing you learning things as you go and along the way, developing the required skill set needed for success. The connections you make along the way not only help support the development of your company but often contribute to helping you become a 'better person' along the way as well. There is often a constant response to unexpected situations which equip you for living in the moment in your life and result in you being more present. You get to personally chose which clients you work with, whom you hire, what partnerships you pursue; you are in complete control of whom you are surrounded with daily. While watching your business blossom and beginning to realize what you are truly capable of, your self-confidence grows substantially—building a company from A to Z fine-tunes all of the leadership traits that can transform you into the most inspiring leader in both professional and personal worlds. You can work wherever you are and while wearing whatever you choose.

No matter what personal or professional reasons you have for pursuing your ventures, I wish you all the luck in the world. I hope this book reminds individuals that there is no truly defined model of the perfect entrepreneur. There are no requirements for becoming an entrepreneur. There are no factors that will strictly determine your success or become an entrepreneur; all factors have positive and negative contributions to these determinations. It is all about your passion, motivation, current economy, idea, planning, innovation, ability to 'sell' yourself, and, most of all, your desire to be a beacon of change for today's ever-changing economy. We need individuals who have been told they are wrong, ill-equipped, or destined to fail to prove the failing rules and norms wrong and pave the road for new age norms. Here is to all entrepreneurs on your venture to create a new world! Thank you for purchasing my book; I hope that I could provide you with some valuable insight and considerations. Please watch for future books- all relating to business consultation, future economic practices, the changing marketplace, advice of revising your 'old' businesses, and more!

You can also access live webinars, recorded webinars, forums, and other resources for all things business at my webpage, where several resources and webinars are offered free of charge.

My company was founded in 2020. The company name is "New Age Business Ventures- The Jacks of Tomorrow". I can be found on Google as well as on a personal webpage. As the business progresses, I will have several more offerings, please feel free to follow me.